THE CLARENDON BIOGRAPHIES
General Editors: C. L. MOWAT and M. R. PRICE

———————

CHARLES DARWIN

by

Robert Olby

Librarian
Botany School, Oxford

OXFORD UNIVERSITY PRESS
1967

Oxford University Press, Ely House, London W.1

GLASGOW NEW YORK TORONTO MELBOURNE WELLINGTON
CAPE TOWN SALISBURY IBADAN NAIROBI LUSAKA ADDIS ABABA
BOMBAY CALCUTTA MADRAS KARACHI LAHORE DACCA
KUALA LUMPUR HONG KONG TOKYO

*Printed in Great Britain by Richard Clay (The Chaucer Press), Ltd.,
Bungay, Suffolk*

CONTENTS

LIST OF PLATES

LIST OF TABLES

TEXT FIGURES

ACKNOWLEDGEMENTS

In the preparation of this biography I have made extensive use of Sir Arthur Keith's *Darwin Revalued*, Lady Barlow's edition of the *Autobiography* and of the *Beagle Diary*, and Professor Woodruff's paper in the *British Medical Journal*. I am indebted to many friends for advice and discussion, and especially to Darwin's grand-daughter, Lady Barlow, to Professor Darlington, Mr. Kenneth Jack, Dr. Erich Posner, and my wife for reading the typescript and making many valuable suggestions. I also wish to record my thanks to Sir Gavin de Beer, Miss Jessie Dobson, Mr. Clulow, Mr. Morice, and Dr. Sidney Smith.

For permission to reprint passages from their publications I am grateful to Messrs. William Collins (pp. 42–43) and to the Editor of the *Notes & Records of the Royal Society* (p. 41). For the originals of the following plates and permission to reproduce them I am grateful to:

The Radio Times Hulton Picture Library—Cover Illustration and Plate 8

Dr. Tellwright, owner of Maer Hall—Plate 1*a*

Messrs. Thames & Hudson—Plate 6

The National Maritime Museum—Plate 1*b*

Mr. Morice—Plate 7*a*

The Royal College of Surgeons—Plates 5*b* and 7*b*

Lady Barlow—Plate 5*a*

I am grateful to Rosemary Wise for the maps, figures, and for Plates 3 and 4.

1

EDUCATION

It is a very odd thing that I have no sensation that I overwork my brain; but facts compel me to conclude that my brain was never formed for much thinking.

THUS wrote the man who had as profound an influence on the course of human thought as did Newton and Aristotle. Darwin was modest about his achievements, candid about his intellect, and only too willing to admit his shortcomings. He had, he declared, 'no great quickness or apprehension or wit', his power to 'follow a long and purely abstract train of thought' was 'very limited', and so poor was his memory that he had 'never been able to remember for more than a few days a single line of poetry'. He recalled that his father, Dr. Robert Waring Darwin, used to say that men with powerful minds generally have memories extending far back to a very early period of life, but Charles could remember no events before 1813, when he was four years of age. Of his mother, who died in 1817, he could remember scarcely anything; but to the end of his days he remembered vividly many details about his father, an imposing figure 6 feet 2 inches tall and weighing 24 stone who was held in awe and reverence by his family. Like his father, Dr. Erasmus Darwin, Dr. Robert worked hard and built up a very flourishing practice at Shrewsbury, thereby adding to the family fortune which, at the time of his death in 1848, must have been worth over a quarter of a million pounds.

Charles regarded his father with great reverence and bowed to his wisdom on most matters. Thus it came about that after leaving Dr. Butler's famous school at Shrewsbury, in 1825, he followed his elder brother Erasmus to Edinburgh University to study medicine. He was sixteen, the schoolboy passion for collecting was still strong with him, and his happy-go-lucky attitude was so persistent that his father declared, 'You care for nothing but shooting, dogs, and rat-catching, and you will be a disgrace to yourself and all your family.'

Charles found the instruction in Edinburgh, which was entirely by lectures, 'intolerably dull'; he attended the meetings of the Royal Medical Society where 'much rubbish was talked', and the lectures of the great geologist Jameson, which determined Darwin 'never as long as I lived to read a book on Geology or in any way to study the science'. Fortunately he soon broke this resolve. When Charles had completed his first year in Edinburgh his brother Erasmus concluded his studies, but he did not go into medical practice. About this time Charles discovered that his father would be leaving him enough money to live on for the rest of his life, a piece of information which gave a decided check to his first earnest efforts to learn medicine. These efforts must have been further discouraged by his sight of two very bad operations performed without chloroform. They haunted him for many years to come.

After two years at Edinburgh it became apparent to his father that Charles was no more likely to enter his profession than was Erasmus. The Doctor must have felt exasperated by this turn of events, but he was determined that Charles should not follow the example of his brother who had become a gentleman of leisure. There was really only one other profession for his sportsman—naturalist son and that was the Church. As a country parson he would have the leisure to continue dabbling in natural history and to indulge in his favourite sport of shooting game. Most of the great names in natural history belonged to the clergy, so here lay hope for the unambitious Charles. Accordingly the Doctor put the suggestion to his son. Charles thought; he read a few theological books; dispersed some doubts about the creed; and gave his consent. As an English degree was necessary he left Edinburgh and, after brushing up his Greek, he entered Christ's College, Cambridge, in December 1827.

Charles did not attempt an Honours course, but keeping well within the limits which his modest industry prescribed, he studied classics, Euclid, algebra, and Paley's *Evidences of Christianity* and his *Moral Philosophy*, for the degree of B.A. Paley's books gave him singular pleasure. He read the *Evidences* so thoroughly that he claimed he could write out the whole book 'with perfect correctness, but not of course in the clear language of Paley'. While admiring the arguments for the existence of God which Paley drew from the evidences of design in nature, he little dreamt that the seeds of doubt would soon be sown in his mind which later would grow into a determination to refute those very arguments.

The three years spent in Cambridge were in Charles' opinion wasted 'as completely as at Edinburgh and at school'. Moreover, he was showing no more enthusiasm for the Church than he had shown for the medical profession. In 1829 he had an earnest conversation with his college friend J. M. Herbert about the question which the Bishop asks in the ordination service: 'Do you trust that you are inwardly moved by the Holy Spirit . . .' Herbert recalled that he could not answer in the affirmative, to which Darwin echoed: 'Neither can I, and therefore I cannot take orders.' One must not read too much into this statement for he soon began thinking about reading divinity, and when away from England in H.M.S. *Beagle*, he looked forward to settling in a quiet country parsonage. Nevertheless, it is clear that already in 1829 he was showing that independence of outlook which prevented him from bowing to orthodoxy whether in matters of religion or of science.

At Cambridge Darwin developed two skills which were later to prove invaluable, collecting beetles and shooting game. He described how in his room at Christ's College he tried to improve his aim either by throwing up his gun in front of a mirror or by getting 'a friend to wave about a lighted candle, and then to fire at it with a cap on the nipple, and if the aim was accurate the little puff of air would blow out the candle. The explosion of the cap caused a sharp crack and I was told that the Tutor of the College remarked, "What an extraordinary thing it is, Mr. Darwin seems to spend hours in cracking a horse-whip in his room, for I often hear the crack when I pass under his windows." '

In January 1831 Darwin sat for the B.A. and passed. He was

tenth in the list of candidates. He had worked just hard enough to do reasonably well. As he had not started the course until the Lent term of 1829 he had to wait until July 1831 before taking his degree. Back in Shropshire for the rest of the summer he worked 'like a tiger' at making a geological map of the county. Then he joined the Cambridge Professor of Geology Adam Sedgwick on his tour through North Wales, and received valuable instruction from the Professor in the art of making geological observations and collecting specimens. But he learnt nothing about glacial action, although they visited the Ogwen valley and spent many hours in the Devil's Kitchen (Cwm Idwal) from which scored rocks, perched boulders, lateral and terminal morains, and U-shaped and hanging valleys, all the results of glacial action, can be clearly perceived. 'A house burnt down by fire did not tell its story more plainly than did this valley,' wrote Darwin eleven years after his Welsh tour.

We have seen that Darwin was not inspired by the formal education of the day. 'No one,' he remarked, 'can more truly despise the old stereotyped stupid classical education than I do.' His reaction to informal education, however, was quite the reverse —he loved it. Botanical excursions with Professor Henslow were among his most treasured memories of student days. He also gained much more from his reading, which was concentrated on travel and the philosophy of science. Two books which had a profound influence on him in his last year at Cambridge were: Humboldt's *Personal narrative of travels to the equinoctial regions of the new continent, during 1799–1804*, and the astronomer John Herschel's *Introduction to the study of natural science*. Darwin also benefited greatly from the teachers he came to know. At Edinburgh and at Cambridge they sought the company of this thoughtful young man, whose greatest merit was that he was a very good listener. Dr. Robert Grant, who was an early convert to evolution, took him to the meetings of the Wernerian Society at Edinburgh. John Henslow (1796–1861), Professor of Botany at Cambridge, befriended him. They dined together and walked together so often that some of the dons called Darwin 'the man who walks with Henslow'. Henslow introduced him to many interesting people in Cambridge, among whom was William Whewell, Master of Trinity College and author of *History of the inductive sciences,* 1837, a book which Darwin much admired.

When he returned home from his geological tour of North Wales on Monday, 29 August 1831, Darwin found two letters awaiting him, one from George Peacock, former Professor of Astronomy at Cambridge, and the other from Professor Henslow. Both letters informed Darwin that he was invited to join Captain Fitz-Roy on his voyage in H.M.S. *Beagle* to South America to survey the coasts of Patagonia, Tierra del Fuego, Chile, Peru, and the South Sea Islands. Darwin was speechless with joy. Ever since reading Humboldt's *Personal narrative of travels* ... he had been longing to visit the tropics, and in the previous spring he had made definite plans with his cousin William Darwin Fox for a trip to Tenerife in June 1832. In the intervening time he started to learn Spanish and fanned his 'Canary ardour' by reading Humboldt over and over again.

Unfortunately Charles' father doubted the wisdom of his son going off on a lengthy voyage, thus putting off the evil day of settling down as a curate. On 30 August Charles wrote to Henslow saying 'my father, although he does not decidedly refuse me, gives such strong advice against going, that I should not be comfortable if I did not follow it'. As we shall see later (p. 48) the stress of going against his father's wish would have been enough to make Charles physically ill. His reply to Mr. Peacock on the same day was therefore a regretful refusal. But Dr. Darwin must have realized how much his son had set his heart on going for he agreed that Charles should seek the opinion of his uncle Josiah Wedgwood. Darwin left next day for 'Maer Hall', the home of 'Uncle Jos', son of old Josiah Wedgwood of Etruria, the founder of the famous pottery firm. Old Josiah and Charles' grandfather, Dr. Erasmus Darwin, had been great friends, so there existed a long-standing friendship between the families. At Maer Hall Charles found the atmosphere more free than at 'The Mount', where the revered Doctor ruled the roost. At Maer, too, there was excellent shooting, and delightful company in the persons of Uncle Jos' four daughters, with whom Charles was a great favourite.

The first evening at Maer was given up to a discussion of Captain Fitz-Roy's offer. Every member of the Wedgwood family was so strongly on Darwin's side that he determined to make another effort to persuade his father to let him go. That evening he drew up a list of the Doctor's objections for Uncle Jos to comment upon. They were as follows:

(1) The voyage would be disreputable to Charles' character as a clergyman and hereafter.

(2) It was a wild scheme.

(3) They must have offered the place of naturalist to many before Darwin.

(4) Since these other candidates had refused the offer 'there must be some serious objection to the vessel or expedition'.

(5) Charles would never settle down to a steady life after the voyage.

(6) The accommodation for the naturalist would be most uncomfortable.

(7) It would constitute a further change of profession.

(8) It would be a useless undertaking.

That same evening Uncle Jos wrote out his opinion of the Doctor's objections in a letter which was 'sent off to Shrewsbury early next morning'. Darwin then went out shooting, but about ten o'clock Uncle Jos sent him a message to say he intended going to Shrewsbury and offered to take Darwin too. When they arrived at the Mount 'all things were settled, and my Father most kindly gave his consent'.

Darwin lost no time but left the following day for Cambridge to say good-bye to Henslow and thence to London where he met Fitz-Roy for the first time on 5 September. Darwin at once took to this handsome, aristocratic, forthright, and youthful captain. Fitz-Roy was twenty-six, only four years older than Darwin. The Captain did not, however, immediately take to Darwin, but did his best to persuade him to defer his decision by emphasizing all the unpleasant aspects of the trip—the cramped quarters, the possibility that they might not sail right round the world. Privately the Captain was having apprehensions about the character of this young naturalist with the pug nose. As an ardent believer in phrenology Fitz-Roy was sure that no man with a nose like Darwin's could have 'sufficient energy and determination for the voyage'. But by the time Darwin had been with Fitz-Roy to visit the ship two weeks later, all was arranged.

Robert Fitz-Roy (1805–65) had been a flag-lieutenant on the previous expedition to South America (1828–30). During the first winter of this expedition he was promoted to the command of the *Beagle* on the death of Captain Stokes. A misfortune which occurred on that trip was indirectly responsible for this second voyage. A party of six men under Mr. Murray's command, who had left the *Beagle* and travelled by whale-boat to Cape Desolation, on the coast of Tierra del Fuego twelve miles from the *Beagle* anchorage, were marooned when the Fuegians stole their boat. They succeeded in constructing a basket with the branches of trees and a portion of their canvas tent, and in this three of the party covered the twelve miles back to the *Beagle* in twenty hours and raised the alarm. As a reprisal a number of hostages were taken, three more Fuegians being obtained voluntarily in exchange for trinkets. All but one of the hostages, 'Boat Memory,' escaped, so that only four Fuegians were brought back to England. Fitz-Roy, with characteristic magnanimity undertook to look after them and return them to Tierra del Fuego as soon as opportunity arose. On their arrival in England they were vaccinated. Fitz-Roy's favourite, Boat Memory, had to be vaccinated four times before the crude technique of those days took effect. Then he became seriously ill and died. The remaining three— York Minster (26),[1] Jemmy Button (14), and Fuegia Basket (9) survived their vaccination and were taken to Walthamstow where an earnest attempt was made to educate and christianize them.

The chief purpose of the 1828–30 expedition to South America had been to survey the east coast from Rio de Janeiro to Cape Horn and to determine the longitude of the former. Since this

[1] Ages estimated in September 1830; they were in England from October 1830 until December 1831.

work had not been completed Fitz-Roy assumed that the Admiralty would send another expedition shortly. But when the Admiralty showed no signs of so doing, Fitz-Roy chartered a vessel himself. This action, together with a little influence in high places, sufficed to change the Admiralty's mind: Fitz-Roy was put in command and given the choice between two ships. He chose the smaller; it was his old well-tried H.M.S. *Beagle*. When the work of refitting it began the hull was found to be so rotten that the whole ship had to be almost completely rebuilt. After raising the height of the upper deck and adding protective sheathing to the hull her weight was 242 tons. She was rigged as a barque, carried six guns, six boats and a dinghy, and lightning conductors on all the masts, bowsprits, and on the flying jib-boom. Every care was taken in her preparation, and Darwin spoke for all the crew when he said: 'She looks most beautiful, even a landsman must admire her. *We* all think her the most perfect vessel ever turned out of the Dockyard. One thing is certain, no vessel has been fitted out so expensively, and with so much care. Everything that can be made so is of mahogany, and nothing can exceed the neatness and beauty of the accommodations.'

Fitz-Roy was thus able to return the Fuegians to their home, and anxious that no opportunity of collecting useful information during the voyage should be lost, he suggested that a 'well-educated and scientific person should be sought for who would willingly share such accommodation as I had to offer, in order to profit by the opportunity of visiting distant countries yet little known'. Captain Beaufort in the Admiralty gladly took up the suggestion, and after consulting with Peacock he invited Leonard Jenyns, 'who was so near accepting it that he packed up his clothes. But having two livings, he did not think it right to leave them ... Henslow himself was not very far from accepting it for Mrs. Henslow most generously and without being asked, gave her consent; but she looked so miserable that Henslow at once settled the point.' He suggested that Darwin should go instead.

All that Fitz-Roy knew about this young man was that he

was a grandson of Dr. Darwin the poet, and 'of promising ability, extremely fond of geology, and indeed all branches of natural history'. He had also been warned by a friend that Darwin was a Whig, but not, of course, that he doubted the Biblical story of creation, for at the beginning of the voyage Darwin was as orthodox a candidate for the Church as one might wish, ready to quote the Bible as the authority on any matter of the day. Thus Fitz-Roy had good grounds for hoping that his naturalist would discover fresh facts from the geology and natural history of South America in support of the biblical story of creation. In early years Fitz-Roy had 'suffered much anxiety ... from a disposition to doubt, if not disbelieve, the inspired history written by Moses'. 'I knew,' he confided, 'so little of that record, or of the intimate manner in which the Old Testament is connected with the New, that I fancied some events there related might be mythological or fabulous, while I sincerely believed the truth of others.... Much of my uneasiness was caused by reading works written by men of Voltaire's school: and by those geologists who contradict, by implication, if not in plain terms, the authenticity of the Scriptures; before I had any acquaintance with the volume which they so incautiously impugne.'

Only when Fitz-Roy read the Bible again with care did he find how true it was. Then he was convinced that the earth was created in seven days, species were created as they now are, the flood came, all were drowned save those in the ark. Fossils are simply the remains of animals drowned by the flood, the relics of an antediluvian (ante = before, diluvian = deluge) age.

Captain Fitz-Roy would have thoroughly approved of the biblical geology which Professor Jameson taught Darwin in Edinburgh. It was basically an adaptation of the Mosaic tradition of the Flood. In the waters of this universal flood all the various materials to be found in the earth's crust were dissolved. Gradually, as the flood began to subside, these dissolved substances crystallized out and were deposited on the bed of this vast sea. Deposition took place in four stages:

(1) Deposition of crystalline layers of *primitive* rocks, such

as granite and basalt upon the original (antediluvian) surface of the earth.

(2) Deposition of crystalline and non-crystalline materials, the latter derived from the erosion of land exposed by the subsiding of the flood. These *transition* rocks were chiefly limestones and slates.

(3) Deposition of the products of further erosion after the flood had retreated to the valleys giving rise to *bedded* rocks, so named on account of their clearly layered structure. Such were chalk, sandstone, coal, and shales, all containing fossils.

(4) Continuing erosion of these deposits have given rise to *alluvial* deposits—sands, gravels, and clays. Volcanic activity was attributed to the burning of vast underground deposits of coal, hence the role of volcanoes in forming deposits was regarded as very minor, and since no volcano could have existed before coal had been deposited, rocks of volcanic origin were all considered to be geologically recent.

Since the supporters of this theory gave to water the chief role in the formation of rocks, they became known as the 'Neptunists'. In opposition to them the 'Vulcanists' gave to volcanic activity the major role. They agreed with the Neptunists that granite and basalt are crystalline, but they held that crystallization takes place from a molten liquid and not from a solution. (In fact, the process by which these rocks are formed is still not perfectly understood, but the Vulcanists' theory was certainly much nearer the truth than was the Neptunists'.)

In addition to emphasizing the importance of volcanic activity the Vulcanists refused to restrict the formation of the grosser details of geological scenery to a remote but fairly brief period around the time of the flood. Why invoke a phase of catastrophes when the work of river, rain, frost, ice, sun, and volcano going on incessantly for hundreds of centuries could achieve as much? Reluctance to accept this view was due not merely to conservatism but to a genuine fear that the biblical time scale would be discarded. If, as the Vulcanist, James Hutton, believed 'there was no trace of a beginning, no vestige of an end', and if the

A Prospect of   Mere Hall

Mr Fowler

Mrs Fowler

Top: Mere (Maer) Hall, the birthplace of Mrs. Darwin.
Above: H.M.S. *Beagle* in the Straits of Magellan.

Fuegia Basket in 1833.   *Jemmy's wife in 1834.*

Jemmy in 1834.   *Jemmy Button in 1833.*

York Minster in 1832.   *York Minster in 1833.*

Natives of Tierra del Fuego. From *Fitz-Roy's Narratives of the Surveying Voyages*

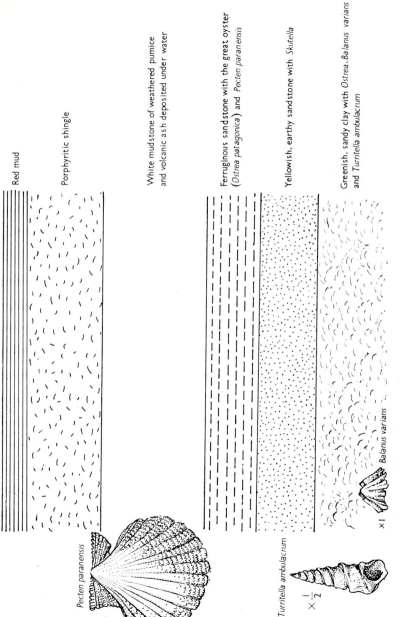

Red mud

Porphyritic shingle

White mudstone of weathered pumice and volcanic ash deposited under water

Ferruginous sandstone with the great oyster (*Ostrea patagonica*) and *Pecten paranensis*

Yellowish, earthy sandstone with *Scutella*

Greenish, sandy clay with *Ostrea*, *Balanus varians* and *Turritella ambulacrum*

Pecten paranensis

×½

Turritella ambulacrum

×½

Balanus varians

×1

Geological deposits revealed at the cliff face of the lowest plain at Port St. Julian.

Geospiza magnirostris

Geospiza strenua

Geospiza fortis

Geospiza parvula

Four of the Finches which Darwin collected in the Galapagos Islands.

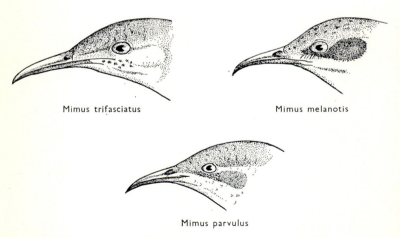

Mimus trifasciatus

Mimus melanotis

Mimus parvulus

The Mocking Birds collected by Darwin from (*left to right*):
Charles, Albermarle, James and Chatham Islands. Redrawn from
The Zoology of the Voyage of H.M.S. Beagle

earth was not a mere 100,000 but several hundred million years old, how could Christians go on believing that the Bible was the inspired word of God?

It was chiefly for these reasons that James Hutton (1726–97) failed in his attempt to establish Vulcanism in the eighteenth century. Hence his views were still sneered at in Darwin's student days. But in 1830 the situation in geology began to change, for it was then that the first volume of Charles Lyell's *The Principles of Geology* appeared. Its author was a young barrister turned geologist, and in this monumental work he sifted the evidence and came out with a massive array of facts in support of Hutton's views. From that time on the Neptunists fought a losing battle.

Henslow had advised Darwin to make geology his study so it was as a geologist rather than as a biologist that Darwin started on the *Beagle* voyage. His parting advice to Darwin was to take a copy of the *Principles* with him on the voyage 'but on no account to accept the doctrine there espoused'. As it turned out, Darwin did not have to buy himself a copy of Volume I because Captain Fitz-Roy gave him one. What irony that so ardent a Christian as the Captain and so devout a naturalist as Henslow should have helped set this young candidate for the Church on the path of doubt which began with disbelief in the geology of Genesis I and led ultimately to agnosticism.

2

VOYAGE ABOARD H.M.S. *BEAGLE*

THE original sailing date of H.M.S. *Beagle* was to have been at the end of September 1831, but by the time the repairs had been completed it was November. Then came the harsh November gales. Twice Fitz-Roy was driven back to Devonport. Not until 27 December 1831, when a favourable east wind sprang up, was the *Beagle* able to sail. Darwin met the Captain and Second Lieutenant for a farewell luncheon of mutton chops and champagne, after which they joined the *Beagle* at 2 p.m. 'Immediately with every sail filled by a light breeze, we scudded away at the rate of 7 or 8 knots an hour.'

In his diary Darwin recorded his disappointment at having to wait so long after all the excitement engendered by the intended swift departure. Those three months were, he said, 'the most miserable which I ever spent, though I exerted myself in various ways. I was out of spirits at the thought of leaving all my family and friends for so long a time, and the weather seemed to me inexpressibly gloomy. I was also troubled with palpitations and pain about the heart....' These pains were probably of neurotic origin; they came first during this enforced idleness, and returned, together with other symptoms again and again in later life (see p. 47).

TABLE I

Principal Dates of the Beagle *Voyage*

1831 27 Dec.	Departure from Devonport	1833–4 Winter	South to Patagonia
1832 16 Jan.	Cape Verde Islands	1834 10 June	Entry to Pacific
28 Feb.	Bahia (Brazil)	27 June	Death of Rowlett, the purser, aged 38
8 Aug.	Monte Video	June 1834 to	
7 Sept.	Bahia Blanca	Sept. 1835	North to Lima
26 Oct.	Monte Video; receives Vol. II of Lyell's *Principles of Geology*	1835 15 Sept.	Galapagos Islands
		9 Nov.	Polynesian Islands
		15 Nov.	Tahiti
1832–3 Winter	Tierra del Fuego; return of captive Fuegians	21 Dec.	New Zealand
		1836 12 Jan.	Australia
1832 22 Dec.	Doubled Cape Horn	29 April	Mauritius
1833 1 March	Falkland Islands	31 May	Cape of Good Hope
Summer	North to Monte Video	8 July	St. Helena
Autumn	Monte Video	1 Aug.	Bahia
		2 Oct.	Falmouth

A delay such as Darwin experienced was not uncommon in those days, for few vessels other than coal barges were powered by steam in the 1830s. So Fitz-Roy had only the wind and the sea for his engines. Sometimes the *Beagle* sped along at 'a rate of knots', sometimes she was becalmed and sometimes she was nearly battered to pieces. Indeed, it is a tribute to her skilful Captain that she returned undamaged, save for the loss of the whale-boat and some of Darwin's collections. And barques such as the *Beagle* were popularly known as 'coffins' on account of their tendency to sink in severe weather.

The chief dates of the voyage are shown in Table I. In this account of the expedition we will confine our attention to Darwin's experiences on the continent of South America (see maps on inside of front and back cover) and the nearby archipelago of the Galapagos Islands (see Fig. 2).

In February 1832 the *Beagle* reached Bahia, a northern port on the Brazilian coast. The view of the city from the Bay of All Saints was magnificent, but to Darwin still more magnificent was the sight of the tropical vegetation. Even Humboldt's descriptions fell short of what Darwin now beheld. In his journal he recorded his feelings as 'a chaos of delights'. 'To a person fond of natural history,' he said, 'such a day as this brings with it pleasure more acute than he ever may again experience.' This intense pleasure in nature was one of the secrets of Darwin's success as a biologist, for it gave him powers of concentration in the act of observing such as are vouchsafed to few men.

As the voyage proceeded, Darwin built up bit by bit the history of the past events which had shaped the continent of South America. Like the crime detective he searched for clues, no matter how trifling and insignificant, in his bid to reconstruct the past. This was the approach to geology which Charles Lyell had expounded in the first volume of his *Principles of Geology*. Darwin had read Volume I in Devonport and was convinced of the superiority of its author's approach over that of his opponents, the Neptunists, before he reached South America. When he had been on that continent a little over a year he received Volume II of the *Principles*, which is devoted to the question of organic evolution.

Although Lyell was convinced that all the diversities of geological phenomena are produced by the long-continued action of natural forces, he could not bring himself to adopt the same attitude to biological phenomena. In the province of the living he did not find changes which are significant for the origin of species. Some species had become extinct, their place had been taken by other species, but the birth of no new species had ever been observed within the period of recorded history. Variations there were, and new breeds of domesticated animals and cultivated plants, but in his view these represented merely the plasticity of the original species, a plasticity held within bounds by the nature of the species. True, some species are more variable than others, but this is merely a provision by the wise Creator to enable some species such as the dog to exist in a greater variety of climates than can other species. Some variability also results from crossing, but this appeared to be temporary, for the progeny of fertile hybrids return or *revert* to one or other of the parental species. The fresh combinations of characters achieved by hybridization Lyell concluded are not lasting. In a similar manner, varieties of domesticated animals and cultivated plants fail to persist in their original form when allowed to run wild. 'It is well known,' wrote Lyell, 'that the horse, the ox, the boar and other domestic animals, which have been introduced into South America, and have run wild in many parts, have entirely lost all marks of domesticity, and have reverted to the original characters of their species.'

Lyell's compromise between recognition of the existence of variability and denial that it is the source of fresh species was the orthodox view at that time.

In the eighteenth century the majority of biologists believed that there was but one centre in which all species arose under the mighty power of the Creator. This we will refer to as the Creation Theory. The discovery of marked differences between the animals and plants of the New World (North and South America) and those of the Old World (Africa, Europe, and Asia), and the unique character of those of Australasia, called for a modification to the belief in a single centre of creation. For if each major land mass, which is cut off from other land masses by an ocean barrier, carries its own characteristic animals and plants, there must have been as many centres of creation as there are isolated major land masses. Either the Creation Theory had to be modified in this way, or it had to be abandoned altogether and diversity in the organic world attributed to a process of change whereby species have arisen progressively, one from another (i.e. evolution). The French biologist J. B. P. Monet de Lamarck (1744–1829) had argued for evolution in his *Philosophie Zoologique*, 1809, and Lyell gave an admirable summary of his argument in the second volume of the *Principles*, while at the same time doing his best to demolish Lamarck's case. Privately Lyell favoured a mutational theory of evolution (see p. 56).

Lamarck believed that all organisms possess the tendency to become, by varying, more complex, thereby rising from one level of organization to a 'higher' level. This tendency to vary is stimulated by the external world whenever there is a change of climate, or of other conditions such as the level of water due to flooding or to drought. These changes in the outside world create 'needs' within the organism. The latter responds by producing appropriate variations. Hence these must of necessity show adaptation to the conditions of life.

Lamarck drew examples from nature on every hand. Thus when a pond dries up, many water plants produce leaves suited to dry conditions which are quite distinct from those formed under water. Europeans who go to the tropics acquire a deep tan to their skins. Lowland plants produce dwarf growth with small leaves when transferred to alpine stations. Hares develop white coats in arctic conditions. Lamarck also knew that the more a man uses his muscles the more powerful they become. So he believed that the giraffe acquired its long neck from stretching up to reach the foliage of tall trees. This is an example of the ancient belief in the inheritance of acquired characters, i.e. that characters acquired during the life of an individual are transmitted to their offspring.

But are characters so acquired really inherited? For centuries people had believed they were, but Lamarck's fanciful treatment of the subject brought it into disgrace. In the fifty years which separate the publication of Lamarck's and Darwin's views on evolution, opinion hardened against both the inheritance of acquired characters and of the slight variations between one individual and another.

Darwin would have nothing to do with Lamarck's book which he referred to as 'veritable rubbish' and 'absurd'. This bias against

Lamarck prevented him from ever realizing how many similari-
ties there are between his and Lamarck's theory.

At the beginning of the voyage Darwin adopted the orthodox
view that species were created at several 'centres', but gradually
his misgivings grew, and by the time he had returned to England his belief in the Creation Theory had been fairly severely
shaken though not destroyed.

Darwin worked hard throughout the voyage. Whenever possible
he explored the hinterland of the coast which the *Beagle* was
charting. If he could travel overland on horseback while the rest
of the crew went by sea, he would. In this way he covered well
over 2,000 miles in South America. No matter how arduous the
ride or dangerous the expedition, nothing deterred him. He was
tough, and thought nothing of weeks of hard riding, attacks of
dysentery, confinement to wretched hovels, and sleeping out in
freezing weather. It required courage, too, to travel long dis-
tances through desolate and arid country where American Indians
lurked. And in the towns of Argentina life was often unsettled,
for revolutions were frequent in this state which had only recently
achieved independence. Darwin counted as many as fourteen
revolutions in twelve months.

Behind the scenes in Argentina the dictatorial General Rosas,
who had formed a Gestapo-like corps, was systematically annihi-
lating his political opponents and maintaining his power by
terror. When Darwin met him in the summer of 1833 he had
resigned his political offices for the time being and was direct-
ing his energies into a war of extermination against the American
Indians of the Cordillera and Pampas. These tribes, unlike their
more peace-loving relations of the Eastern seaboard, had become increasingly troublesome to the more outlying Estancias
(ranches) and to Patagones and Bahia Blanco—at that time the
only settlements of civilized man south of Buenos Aires. Darwin described the General's plan in his *Journal*. Briefly it was to
drive these western tribes to a common point and attack them
in a body, repeating this operation for three consecutive years.
Those eastern tribes who had come to fight for Rosas were also
to be reduced in number, for the General, 'like Lord Chester-

field, thinking that his friends may in a future day become his enemies, always places them in the front ranks, so that their numbers may be thinned'.

This fearful and bloody battle waged by one race against another left a strong impression on Darwin, and we may suspect that it made him realize how effective is the struggle for existence in eliminating one race and establishing another.

When the *Beagle* reached the collection of wild islands south of the Straits of Magellan, called Tierra del Fuego 'Land of Fire' (so named by Magellan in 1550 on account of the numerous fires which the Fuegians lit at the sight of his ship) Darwin came face to face for the first time with savage man. 'I shall never forget,' he said, 'how wild and savage one group appeared: suddenly four or five men came to the edge of an overhanging cliff; they were absolutely naked, and their long hair streamed about their faces; they held rugged staffs in their hands, and, springing from the ground, they moved their arms round their heads, and sent forth the most hideous yells.'

There were several tribes of these copper-coloured people, each separated from their neighbours by the natural barriers of mountain, sea, and river, or by a neutral territory the crossing of which brought with it bloody battle. The Fuegians on the west coast wore cloaks of guanaco skins (the guanaco is the wild llama), those on the east coast seal skins, and the central tribes otter skins 'or some small scrap about as large as a pocket handkerchief, which is barely sufficient to cover their backs as low down as their loins. It is laced across the breast by strings, and according as the wind blows, it is shifted from side to side.' But the most miserable Fuegians that Darwin saw were quite naked. One woman, who was suckling her new-born child, 'came one day alongside the vessel, and remained there out of curiosity, whilst the sleet fall and thawed on her naked bosom, and on the skin of her naked baby. These poor wretches were stunted in their growth, their hideous faces bedaubed with white paint, their skins filthy and greasy, their hair entangled, their voices discordant, and their gestures violent.' Their wigwams were no larger than a haycock and consisted 'of a few broken branches stuck in the ground, and very imperfectly thatched on one side with a few tufts of grass and rushes'. Darwin estimated that 'the whole cannot be the work of an hour, and it is only used for a few days'. Usually these primitive men slept out naked on the wet cold ground in huddles of five or six, coiled up like animals.

Fuegian men usually had two wives. While the men acted as warriors protecting the tribe and hunting guanaco, otters, and seals, their wives toiled incessantly from morning until night, rearing children, collecting shellfish, and a fungus growing on beech trees (*Cyttaria darwinii*), and the berries of the dwarf strawberry tree, or they dived for sea eggs or, sitting 'patiently in their canoes, and with a baited hair line without any hook', they jerked out little fish. This meagre diet was supplemented from time to time with seals, porpoises, otters, and the occasional rotting carcass of a whale. When food was scarce the elder women were said to suffer a terrible death—suffocation over a smoke fire, followed by roasting and consumption by the rest of the tribe. Darwin forecast that if the sea food upon which he so largely depended were to perish, 'the Fuegian savage, the miserable lord of this miserable land, would redouble his cannibal feasts, decrease in numbers, and perhaps cease to exist'.[1]

The miserable state of the Fuegians prompted Darwin to ask: 'What could have tempted, or what change compelled a tribe of men, to leave the fine regions of the north, to travel down the Cordillera or backbone of America, to invent and build canoes, which are not used by the tribes of Chile, Peru, and Brazil, and then to enter on one of the most inhospitable countries within the limits of the globe?' There is little doubt that the key phrase in this passage is, 'or what change compelled', for surely nothing less than the will to survive in the face of attacks by more powerful northern races could have led these tribes into so terrible a climate. And once there the battle for survival went on unremittingly. If one tribe ran out of food it attacked a neighbour-

---

[1] According to E. Lucas Bridges, *Uttermost Part of the Earth*, Hodder & Stoughton, 1948, these tribes were nothing like as primitive as Darwin and Fitz-Roy believed.

survival
of the
fittest

ing tribe. 'The cause of their warfare,' said Darwin, 'appears to be the means of subsistence.' Thus did these Fuegians provide Darwin with a vivid example of the battle for survival which is going on every day in the realm of nature.

Despite the suspicious and at times threatening behaviour of the Fuegians, Captain Fitz-Roy succeeded in returning his charges to their native country, landing them at Woollȳa Bay, the home of Jemmy's tribe (see map at end of book). Jemmy Button did not enjoy this experience and wanted to return to the ship, but on being given a wife he decided to stay. York Minster married Fuegia Basket and the couple left for York's home at Christmas Sound.

Fitz-Roy was unsuccessful in establishing a missionary station at Woollȳa Bay. Young Richard Matthews, who had been selected by the Church Missionary Society for this difficult assignment, was very lucky to have survived the ten days until the *Beagle* returned to see how he was getting on. The situation looked so grave that Matthews had to be taken back on board. Of the odd collection of equipment provided for him by the missionary society—butter bolts, wine glasses, tea-trays, soup tureens, mahogany dressing case, fine white linen, beaver hats, &c.—hardly anything remained. He had been menaced day and night and would soon have been killed had the crew of the *Beagle* left him to the Fuegians' mercy. Thus ended the attempt to establish a mission in Tierra del Fuego. The wigwams which the ship's crew had built, the gardens they had prepared, and the seeds they had sown were left to go to ruin. The only appreciation of Fitz-Roy's efforts came from poor Jemmy. He had tried, he explained, to keep his tribe from walking over the garden, but they did not heed him. Day after day he had watched for the sprouting of the peas, beans, and other vegetables, but in vain. He gave the Captain and another member of the crew an otter skin each, two spear-heads which had been made 'expressly for Mr. Darwin' and a bow and quiver full of arrows for his schoolmaster in Walthamstow.

The most important fact about the southern part of this continent which Darwin discovered was its comparatively recent origin. The 1,200 miles of coastline between the Rio Plata and Tierra del Fuego, he reckoned, had been raised above sea-level *en masse* during the early Tertiary era (now estimated to be 70–50 million years ago). The total elevation of the Patagonian plateau had been about 1,000 feet, but owing to eight lengthy intermissions in the progress of this uprising, the sea had had time to wear away and level out the rising land, thus giving rise to eight step-wise plateaux, four of which are shown in Text Figure 1.

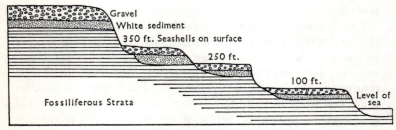

Fig. 1. The Plateaux of Patagonia

Darwin's estimate of the age of the Patagonian plateau was based on the presence throughout its coastline of deposits rich in shells of species of molluscs which are still abundant in the adjacent coastal waters today. These fossiliferous deposits together with the more recent strata laid down upon them were exposed to Darwin's view in the coastal cliffs. Their arrangement at Port St. Julian is illustrated in Plate 4.

To the Captain's way of thinking the structure of these coastal cliffs was not due to a gradual accumulation of shells and deposition of the products of weathering of existing rocks, followed by a gradual elevation of the sea-bed. On the contrary it resulted from a sudden catastrophe—the flood. The compacted state of the fossils throughout these cliffs was for Fitz-Roy adequate evidence 'that Patagonia was once under the sea; that the sea grew deeper over the land in a tumultuous manner, rushing to and fro, tearing up and heaping together shells which once grew regularly or in beds; that the depth of water once became so great as to squeeze or mass the earth and shells together by its enormous pressure; and that after being so forced down, the cohesion of the mass became sufficient to resist the separating power of other waves, during the subsidence of that ocean which had overwhelmed the land'. Furthermore Fitz-Roy was convinced that if Patagonia was flooded to so great a depth, then all the world must have been under water. '. . . and from these shells alone,' he declared, 'my own mind is convinced (independently of the Scriptures) that this earth has undergone a universal deluge.'

To Darwin the history of these cliffs read very differently. They had indeed been the bed of a former sea, but at the time of the deposition of these fossiliferous beds, not a deep sea, for the shells in question belonged to shallow-water species. Nor did the conditions under which deposition took place appear to have been violent, for the various fossil vertebrates which Darwin found in these cliffs showed no disturbance of the relative positions of the bones in the skeleton. Undulations in the boundary between adjacent strata, moreover, were very like the irregularities produced by wave action on a beach or shallow sea-bed.

The evidences which Darwin found in the Cordillera pointed in the same direction: volcanic activity of the sea-bed giving rise to extensive submarine lavas, accumulation upon these lavas of sedimentary deposits, elevation of these deposits and lavas to a height of about 14,000 feet above sea-level. Of the two principal ridges of the Cordillera, the Pequenes and the Portillo, Darwin judged the former to be the older despite its lower altitude, for it formed the main east–west watershed, rivers which flow to the east having cut through the Portillo ridge at a time when this ridge was lower than the Pequenes. The shells in the Pequenes belonged to the secondary era, to the early cretaceous (now estimated as about 130,000,000 years ago). The elevation of the Cordillera must thus have begun before that of the Tertiary deposits of Patagonia.

During the elevation of the Cordillera there had, in Darwin's opinion, been lengthy periods of rest, when the weathering of exposed rocks yielded immense quantities of sedimentary deposits.

Captain Fitz-Roy, on the other hand, preferred to attribute the huge size of these deposits to the action of immense forces heaping them up rather than to a lengthy period of gradual accumulation. Thus the alternating layers of sedimentary and volcanic rocks which Darwin found in the Cordillera at a height of 8,000–9,000 feet were for the Captain 'proofs of that tremendous castrophe which alone could have caused them;—of that awful combination of waters and volcanic agency which is shadowed forth to our minds by the expression "the fountains of the great deep were broken up, and the windows of heaven were opened" '.

Darwin's last proof of the gradual elevation of this continent was his observation of an increase in height of the coast at Concepcion as a result of an earthquake which he himself experienced in March 1835. Successive small uprisings of this sort accompanied by an imperceptibly slow rise of the land, he held, would lead in the course of time to considerable elevation.

Darwin's observations of the animals and plants of South America, unlike his geological observations, did not at once yield material for building theories. Only after he had returned home and had begun an extensive programme of reading did the knowledge he gained on the voyage fit together into a theory of adaptive evolution.

The most curious aspect of the biology of South America is the contrast between the animals of that continent and those of Africa. Genera which are rich in species on the continent of Africa tend to be poorly represented in South America, and vice versa. And why are the savannas of Africa so richly stocked with large mammals while comparable tracts of South America support little else besides guanaco, and the occasional vicuna, puma, jaguar, and deer? The great French naturalist, Georges Louis Leclerc de Buffon (1707–88), simply concluded that the creative force in South America had never possessed much vigour. But he could not know that the relics of a former age rich in giant mammals lay hidden in the ground. Some of these fossils were exposed in cliff faces and on beaches. At Punta Alta, Darwin found nine different fossil mammals scattered over 200 square yards of beach. Clearly this region of South America must have supported a large number of these mammals at a not very remote period. From Punta Alta, the Rio Negro, and the Santa Cruz, Darwin brought to England the fossil remains of a total of eleven species of extinct mammalia. Their names and affinities are given in Table II.

The greater part of 1834 and 1835 was spent travelling up the west coast of South America. During these years Darwin studied the geology of the Andes in some detail and arrived at his theory of their origin. In September 1835 the *Beagle* reached the Galapagos Archipelago, a collection of ten principal islands situated about 600 miles west of Ecuador. All the islands in the group are volcanic in origin and Darwin estimated that there must be about 2,000 extinct craters in the whole archipelago. The unworn state of these craters and the clear margins to the lava streams convinced him of the recent origin of the Galapagos.

TABLE II

Extinct Mammals found by Darwin in South America

Fossil Genus	Similar live forms	Place of find	Parts found
Glossotherium	Armadilloes	Rio Salada	Part of the cranium
Scelidotherium	Cape ant-eater	Punta Alta	Nearly complete skeleton
Mylodon	(Between) armadilloes and sloths	Punta Alta	Lower jaw with teeth
Megalonyx	Sloths	Punta Alta	Lower jaw with 1 tooth
Megatherium	Sloths	Punta Alta	Part of cranium and 5 molar teeth
Glyptodon	Armadilloes	Punta Alta	Portion of boney armour
Mastodon	Elephant	Rio Parana	Fragments of molar teeth
Equus	Horse	Punta Alta	One molar tooth
Macrauchenia	(Between) guanaco and horse	Port St. Julian	Several vertebrae and limb bones
Toxodon	(Between) capybara and sloths	Punta Alta	Fragment of lower jaw with teeth
		Rio Salado	Cranium
Ctenomys	Tucutucu	Monte Hermoso	Fragment of upper jaw with two molars
Hydrochoerus	Capybara	Monte Hermoso	Head of femur and fragments of pelvic bones

The dates of these finds were as follows: Rio Salado and Parana 1.10.33; Punta Alta 22.9.32; 8 and 16.10.32; Port St. Julian 9.1.34; Monte Hermoso 19.10.33.

When Darwin landed he was greeted by a 'strange Cyclopean scene'. The rocks of black lava, the almost leafless shrubs, the large cacti, the great lumbering tortoises and the ugly lizards resembling strongly an antediluvian scene. Strange and grotesque reptiles unknown anywhere else in the world dominated these islands. Darwin reckoned that only one of the 26 species of land birds, one of the 16 kinds of land shells, and three of the 25 species of beetles which he found there occur elsewhere. In the plant kingdom the proportion of unique species was not so high. Out of a total of 185 species of flowering plants 10 were probably introduced by man, 85 reached the archipelago by other means and the remaining 100 species are found nowhere else.

Darwin had been in the Galapagos for about ten days before he met the Vice-Governor, Mr. Lawson, who told him that the tortoises differed in character from island to island and that he could with certainty tell from which island any one was brought. Darwin took little note of this comment for he 'never dreamed that islands, about fifty or sixty miles apart, and most of them in sight of each other, formed of precisely the same rocks, placed under a quite similar climate, rising to a nearly equal height, would have been differently tenanted'. But on comparing the specimens of mocking-thrushes (*Mimus*) collected from four islands he was astonished to discover that the three species obtained were confined to three island groups as follows:

Mimus trifasciatus, Charles Island.

M. *parvulus*, Albemarle Island.

M. *melanotis*, James and Chatham Islands (these two are linked by intermediate islands).

Now his attention was 'thoroughly aroused', but he had already mixed up the specimens of finches collected from Chatham and Charles Islands. Fortunately those shot on James Island had been kept separate, so he was able to demonstrate that two species of finch found on James Island were not found on Chatham and Charles Islands and two species found on the latter were not found on the former. Darwin brought back a total of thirteen species of these strange finches which showed 'a nearly perfect gradation of structure ... in the form of the beak, from one exceeding in dimensions that of the largest gros-beak, to another differing but little from that of a warbler'. And in the *Journal and Remarks* which he wrote in 1837–8 he added: 'I very much suspect that certain members of the series are confined to different islands.'

Darwin went to great pains to make a good collection of plants from the Galapagos. 'I indiscriminately collected everything in

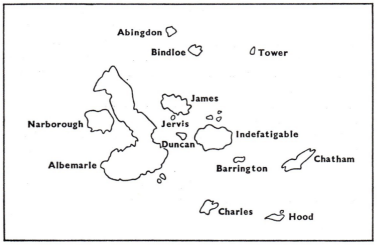

Fig. 2. The Galapagos Islands

flower on the different islands, and fortunately kept my collections separate.' This enabled Dr. Joseph Hooker, who was later to become Darwin's closest friend, to work out the extent of the isolation of the flora of four of the islands.

After spending a month in the Galapagos the *Beagle* sailed for New Zealand. Then she made tracks for home via the circuitous route: Australia–South Africa–Brazil–Falmouth. In the winter of 1835–6 Darwin had the opportunity to reflect on his South American and Galapagos discoveries. The great question which haunted him was why one Creator should fashion different forms to fill identical niches in the economy of nature. For instance, why were identical habitats on the east and west sides of the Cordillera occupied by different animals and plants? Why not use the same form for the same purpose everywhere? Why furnish the finch group as well as the warbler group with an insect-eating beak, the finch group in addition to the wood-pecker group with a wood-boring beak, and so on? This pheno-menon is now called 'Parallel Evolution', and Darwin en-countered it again in Australia where he found marsupials occupy-ing habitats which on other continents are the province of mam-mals. In his diary he commented that an irrational person might exclaim, 'Surely two distinct Creators must have been at work,' but he himself was convinced that there was only 'the one hand'. On the long journey back from Australia these cases of parallel evolution haunted him and he pondered on how the 'Disbeliever' would view them.

Thus by the time the *Beagle* returned to England in October 1836 Darwin had called in question the Creation Theory no matter how modified to fit the facts. But he had no intention of being indiscreet or hurried over so important a subject as the origin of species. He would be patient and bide his time. Mean-while he could see no useful purpose in abandoning the Creation Theory until a plausible alternative were found.

3

THE BIRTH OF A THEORY

WHEN Darwin presented himself at Shrewsbury in October 1836 after an absence of five years and two days his father turned to Charles' sisters and declared: 'Why, the shape of his head is quite altered.' The characteristic flattening of the back of his head, the firm jaw, pug nose, beetling eyebrows, and nob-shaped chin were now much more noticeable than they had been when he left England at the age of twenty-three. He had also changed in other ways. From the easy-going, cheerful, and sociable fellow

Darwin with his
son William.

Darwin's Study at Down.

The Sand Walk.

Top: Dr. Gully's Health Establishment at Malvern.
Above: Part of Darwin's health diary.

Darwin—the last picture taken before his death.

of twenty-three he had become the purposeful naturalist of twenty-eight who could not abide to waste an hour, who had developed a taste for 'building theories and accumulating facts in silence and solitude'. He admitted that throughout the five years of the voyage, 'the whole of my pleasure was derived from what passed in my mind while admiring views by myself, travelling across the wild deserts or glorious forests or pacing the deck of the poor little *Beagle* at night'.

Back in his homeland Darwin found himself already a famous man. He was no longer the 'man who walks with Henslow' but the naturalist of the *Beagle* whose informative letters to Henslow had been read in November 1835 to the Cambridge Philosophical Society and printed as a pamphlet for distribution among its members and whose fine scientific collections were the talk of the day. Such a man found at once a ready entrance into scientific circles and had little difficulty in persuading the experts of the day to collaborate with him in the great work of describing the fruits of the voyage.

After Shrewsbury, Darwin's next objective was Cambridge where Henslow had charge of all his collections. First he sorted his large collection of minerals with the help of the Professor of Mineralogy. This task completed he left for London where he found accommodation in a house a few doors away from his brother Erasmus in Great Marlborough Street. There he set to work on his journal, copying it out and adding to it for his contribution to the official *Narrative of the Surveying Voyages of H.M.S. 'Adventure' and 'Beagle'*, volume iii. Within three months he had completed it, but it was another year before it was published. A comparison of this work with the manuscript journal will show that Darwin did a lot of research into the history of South America during these three months, in order to establish what changes in the flora and fauna had taken place since the arrival of Europeans in the fifteenth and sixteenth centuries. Many an hour must he have spent in the British Museum poring over the reports of earlier voyages. One striking example of biological change which he discussed deserves mention here, that occasioned by the introduction of the horse to South America.

C

The first horses were landed at Buenos Ayres in 1537. In 1580, only forty-three years later, horses were reported from as far away as the Straits of Magellan. Evidently these quadrupeds had run wild and bred rapidly. Even in 1580 American Indians were seen to be using horses, and by Darwin's time only the Fuegians, cut off from the mainland by the Straits of Magellan, were without them. This success of the European horse is strange considering that South America once possessed its own native horse, a fossil tooth of which Darwin brought back to England. To him it was a marvellous fact 'that in South America a native horse should have lived and disappeared, to be succeeded in after ages by the countless herds descended from the few introduced by the Spanish colonists!'

Darwin's *Journal and Remarks* . . . (1839) was not only the most popular of the 3-volume official report of the *Voyages of H.M.S. 'Adventure' and 'Beagle'*, it was also Darwin's most readable book. About 200,000 words in length it continued to sell steadily for many years. The second edition entitled *Journal of Researches* . . . (1845) has recently been reprinted as a paperback. Next he turned to the geology of the voyage and by 1846 he had written three books: *Coral Reefs, Geological observations on South America*, and *Volcanic Islands*. In these works he gave the detailed evidence for his assertion of the recent elevation of much of the continent of South America and for his theory of the origin of coral reefs. As the former subject has already been described on pp. 26–28 we will concern ourselves here only with the latter. The great merit of this theory, as with his theory of natural selection, was that it explained such a wide range of observations—those made on all three basic types of reef: atoll, fringing, and barrier reef.

The early mariners fancied that coral-building animals instinctively built up their great circles to afford themselves protection in the inner parts. This notion was superseded by the theory that coral activity develops on the rim of a crater in the sea-bed, this being the crater of a submarine volcano. On this theory all atolls ought to be approximately round, and of the same range in diameter as is found among terrestrial volcanoes. But many atolls have an immense diameter and are highly irregular in shape. According to a third theory the ring-shaped character of atolls is due to the greater rate of growth of the coral on the exposed side to that on the protected side, thus giving rise to a cup-shaped structure.

None of these theories, however, could account for the fact that a reef many hundreds of feet thick could have been pro-

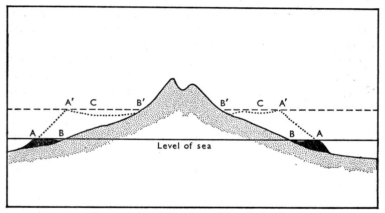

Fig. 3. The Formation of Coral Islands*

duced by organisms which can only live to a depth of between twenty and thirty fathoms.[1]

Darwin's studies on the continent of South America had made him very aware of the effects of subsidence and elevation of land masses. Could it be, he thought, that a simple fringing reef develops in the shallow water surrounding an island. The island sinks, taking the reef with it. As it sinks the coral continues to build upon its base of dead calcareous shells, thus forming a great bank of coral with water on either side (see Fig. 3). Thus an island which starts with a fringing reef will gradually diminish in size as it sinks, leaving a barrier reef around it. Finally it will

[1] Captain Fitz-Roy arrived at this figure from his soundings on Keeling Atoll.

* AA = fringing reef; BB = island shores; AA′ = conversion of fringing reef into barrier reef after subsidence of the land; BB′ = island shores after subsidence; CC = lagoon channel.

disappear altogether, leaving only the reef above water as an atoll.

This coral island theory was not tested experimentally before being launched. A year before his death Darwin wrote to a friend: 'I wish that some doubly rich millionaire would take it into his head to have borings made in some of the Pacific and Indian atolls.' When this suggestion was taken up, the first results were inconclusive. But since the use of Bikini Atoll as a nuclear-testing site, detailed studies of the atoll's foundations have been made. Coral was brought up from borings which reached a depth of 2,556 feet, and seismic exploration beneath the lagoon indicated a platform of hard rock at least 8,000 feet below. Here was the evidence which Darwin had wanted. His view that coral islands are produced by the submergence of land coupled with the building activity of coral is now well proven. What is not so clear is how the rock underlying atolls comes to be so near the surface, for generally it is not in the form of a subterranean mountain but a platform. Hence it seems doubtful that all three types of island can be put into one series; an atoll may not necessarily be the successor of a coral island with barrier reef.

Darwin's coral island theory brought him instant fame among scientists long before he won renown as a biologist. It also transformed his acquaintance with Lyell into a lasting friendship. Writing to Darwin's former teacher Adam Sedgwick in April 1837, Lyell said: 'It is rare even in one's own pursuits to meet with congenial souls; and Darwin is a glorious addition to my society of geologists, and is working hard and making way both in his book and in our discussions. I really never saw that bore —Dr. Fitton—so successfully silenced, or such a bucket of cold water so dexterously poured down his back as when Darwin answered some impertinent and irrelevant questions about South America.'

Darwin's work on the elevation of South America and on coral islands formed only part of his geological studies during the voyage. He also made important contributions to our knowledge of petrology (origin, structure, and composition of rocks). He believed that when cooling rock crystallizes the more basic crystals form first and sink through the more acidic molten rock, thus affecting a separation between basic and acidic constituents. He was also the first to distinguish clearly between stratification, due to the manner of deposition, and what he termed 'foliation' (like the layered structure of leaf mould), due to the direction of flow of the molten rock as it recrystallizes. His geological work, like his biological studies, is as rich in detailed observations as it is with theoretical conclusions.

Today we are well accustomed to accept the view that the surface of the earth has been greatly modified by the action of water, heat, cold, and ice. But at the time of the *Beagle* voyage the immensity of these forces of denudation was little appreciated. Darwin's *Journal* gave to its wide audience vivid pictures of these forces at work. The roar of mountain streams 'spoke eloquently' to Darwin of the thousands and thousands of stones which are striking against each other, and he remarked: 'As often as I have seen beds of mud, sand and shingle, accumulated to the thickness of many thousand feet, I have felt inclined to exclaim that causes such as the present rivers and the present beaches could never have ground down and produced such masses. But, on the other hand, when listening to the rattling noise of these torrents, and calling to mind that whole races of animals have passed away from the face of the earth, and that during this whole period, night and day, these stones have gone rattling onward on their course, I have thought to myself can any mountains, any continent withstand such waste?'

We have seen that during the voyage Darwin began to question the theory of centres of creation, but he did not abandon it. He was 'deeply impressed' by the great fossils with armour like that of existing armadilloes, by the distribution of South American animals—closely related forms replacing one another as one proceeds southwards, and 'by the South American character of most of the productions [i.e. organisms] of the Galapagos archipelago, and more especially by the manner in which they differ slightly on each island of the group; none of the islands appearing to be very ancient in a geological sense'. These facts could only be satisfactorily explained on the assumption that species are evolved

gradually. Why, then, did Darwin not accept evolution during
the voyage? Because he could see no advantage in so doing until
a plausible explanation could be found for the beautiful adaptation of organisms to their respective habitats. Lamarck's opinion
that when an organism feels an *inner need* for an organ which it
lacks, in order to obtain food, escape the hunter, and so on, it is
able to develop that organ, was in Darwin's opinion quite inadequate to account for beautiful adaptations such as those of
the woodpecker and tree frog to tree climbing, and the hooked
and plumed seeds to seed dispersal. He had always been struck,
he said, 'by such adaptations, and until these could be explained
it seemed to me almost useless to endeavour to prove by indirect
evidence that species have been modified'.

As he sorted his collections and prepared his journal for publication he 'then saw how many facts indicated the common descent
of species'. There must, he thought, be some mechanism by
which slight variations are accumulated generation by generation
so that organisms at first identical can in the course of time come
to differ widely.

In March 1837 Darwin moved to Great Marlborough Street,
London. The first two years he spent at this address were the
most momentous in his life. First he re-read Lyell's *Principles
of Geology*, this time in the fifth edition, which had just been
published. Dr. Sidney Smith of St. Catherine's College, Cambridge, has recently pointed out that Darwin made scarcely any
notes in the first edition of this book when he read it on the
voyage. But in March 1837 no passage bearing on the question of
evolution escaped a critical comment from Darwin's pencil. Here
for the first time he was putting forward 'my theory' as a more
satisfactory explanation of the facts than the old theory of centres
of creation. At this time it would seem that 'my theory' was that
variation in nature has no limits, it is inherited and can thus be
accumulated generation by generation. Therefore species possess
the capacity to change, and if the slight variations which they
show prove advantageous to them, then they will be preserved.
The result will be the production of new forms *adapted* to their
habitats. This hypothesis was not at this stage worked out in any

detail, and the struggle for existence appears to have played no part in it. But this hypothesis looked promising, so he decided to collect facts wherever he could which might throw light on the subject. He conversed with breeders and gardeners, he sent out circulars asking for information about variation, he read widely, very widely—'When I see the list of books of all kinds which I read and abstracted, including whole series of journals and transactions, I am surprised at my industry,' he wrote. But he soon realized 'that selection was the keystone of man's success in making useful races of animals and plants'. How, then, does nature select?

Being a methodical man, Darwin made a definite plan and stuck to it—he started a series of notebooks on evolution. His diary records: 'In July opened first notebook on Transmutation of Species. Had been greatly struck from about month of previous March on character of S. American fossils—and species on Galapagos Archipelago.—These facts origin (especially latter) of all my views.' However important the day nothing deterred him, not even the first day of married bliss prevented him from jotting down an idea in his notebook when it came into his head.

By the autumn of 1838 he had perceived that competition between species or the 'struggle for existence' gives the situation in which individuals slightly better adapted to their surroundings than the remainder of the population would get the upper hand and in the course of time form a new species. Now he was beginning to see how nature selects. But how effective would this sort of selection be?

While he was thinking on these lines he was also reading a variety of books 'for amusement'. Among his list of 'light reading' we find *An essay on the principles of population,* by Thomas Robert Malthus (1766–1834). In this famous book Malthus attacked the social reformers who believed that by improving the lot of the poor and the unfortunate a future age of universal happiness would result. Such was the view of his father's circle of friends and Malthus rejected it passionately. For to him man was at heart a lazy creature who would only work if driven to it. What had driven man to rise from the savage state? What impelled him to clear the forest and plant crops? The answer was simple—the fear of starvation. Nature assures the continuing presence of this fear by endowing man and the brute creation with the capacity for reproduction greatly in excess of the available food supply. This law of nature he expressed succinctly in the phrase: 'Population, when unchecked, increases in a geometrical ratio. Subsistence [i.e. food] increases only in an arithmetical ratio.' He could see 'no way by which man can escape from the weight of this law which pervades all animate nature. No fancy equality, no agrarian regulations, in their utmost extent, could remove the pressure of it, even for a single century.' Thus if the reproductive rate in man would yield double the population in twenty-five years, it would increase it four times in fifty years and sixteen times in a century. The production of food, on the other hand, would be increased only eight times in a century.

The brute creation, because it lacks the ability to think ahead, continues to reproduce at the maximum rate regardless of the consequences. The result is the death of many and the survival of few. But man can foresee the burdens which he will heap upon himself when he marries and raises a family. Hence for the man of small means Malthus' advice was either to postpone marriage until he could afford it, or to remain single.

Malthus lived in an age which knew virtually nothing of social welfare and he wished it to remain that way. For if one were to increase the food supply and improve the lot of the poor, he reasoned, they would then bring more children into the world, and again there would be insufficient food to go round. Or suppose the population be kept well within the limits set by the food supply. Then man would just be more idle and he would go on being idle until a severe shortage of food developed. A deliberate check to population growth would remove the stimulus to man's productive efforts. No, there was only one answer—*laissez faire*—leave things as they are. Allow nature to do the checking and supply the impetus to man's endeavours.

The kindly Darwin must have been nearly as shocked by Malthus' complacent advocacy of this harsh social theory as we are today. But he did not for a moment question the existence of these natural checks, examples of which Malthus had described so vividly.

We used a period of twenty-five years in our illustration of the working of Malthus' law. In fact, Malthus had asserted that the human population would double itself in a *far shorter time*, if all offspring survived. This assertion impressed Darwin greatly and made him realize how powerful are the natural checks to man's increase. He described these checks as a 'force like a hundred thousand wedges trying [to] force every kind of adapted structure into the gaps in the economy of nature or rather forming gaps by thrusting out weaker ones'. Now he was convinced that the struggle for existence has far-reaching consequences. Failure of individuals to survive may mean the extinction of the species. Success of individuals deviating from the type may lead to the production of a new species. Darwin termed this the Principle of Natural Selection. It requires three assumptions:

(1) heritable variations occur in nature;
(2) there is a struggle for existence;
(3) forms better suited to their surroundings survive at the expense of other forms.

We may summarize the steps by which Darwin arrived at this hypothesis as follows:

(1) there is no limit to variation;
(2) man selects and accumulates variations suited to his needs in his domesticated animals and cultivated plants;
(3) in nature 'favourable' variations get the upper hand in the struggle for existence;
(4) This struggle for existence is so intense that ill-adapted forms become extinct and well-adapted forms give birth to new species.

Darwin was twenty-nine when he made this discovery. To us it may seem a simple idea that does not require long and intense thought to develop. But the fact remains that in Darwin's day only three writers (see p. 56) had got farther than appreciating that the struggle for existence has led to the extinction of certain species. This we may term the 'negative aspect' of natural selection. Lyell appreciated this and he believed further that new species are produced to fill the gaps left by the extinct species, but the question of 'how' he left unanswered. To move from Lyell's position to Darwin's was not accomplished easily the first time; to grasp the 'positive aspect' of selection called for an original piece of thinking. Darwin achieved this quite independently of the three writers who had done it before him. We may well ask: Why did these three writers not seize their opportunity and exploit it? Surely because they appreciated its importance only very dimly. None of them wrote a book about it or made any attempt to collect precise information with which to support it. Darwin, on the other hand, studied nature assiduously, fully realizing what a great principle is natural selection. He knew that if accepted, evolution by natural selection would rend biology from top to bottom.

When Darwin read 'Malthus' he had been back in England two years. The immediate labours connected with the harvest from his voyage were over. He was almost out of his twenties. It was high time he decided what sort of a career to follow and to stick to it. Should he aim at a Cambridge professorship or should he remain a gentleman of leisure in London and make summer tours? Should he concentrate on zoology or on geology? Should he marry or remain single? He wrote out all the *pros* and *cons* on two scraps of paper which have miraculously survived to this day. The second paper is headed 'This is the Question' and below are two columns entitled 'MARRY' and 'Not MARRY'. Under 'MARRY' we find: 'My God, it is intolerable to think of spending one's whole life, like a neuter bee, working, working, working and nothing after all. No, no won't do.—Imagine living all one's days solitary in smoky dirty London House.—Only picture to yourself a nice soft wife on a sofa with good fire, and books and music perhaps—compare this vision with the dingy reality of Grt. Marlborough St. Marry—Marry—Marry Q.E.D.'

The prospect worried him none the less. There would be such a loss of time involved in receiving and visiting relations; he might not have sufficient money to buy the books he wanted, and if he had a large family he might be forced to earn his living. Then there were his financial affairs—how would he manage them all if he were obliged to go walking with his wife every day. 'Eheu!! I never should know French,—or see the Continent,—or go to America, or go up in a balloon, or take solitary trips in Wales—poor slave, you will be worse than a Negro—and then horrid poverty (without one's wife was better than an angel and had money)—Never mind my boy—Cheer up—One cannot live this solitary life, with groggy old age, friendless and cold and childless staring one in one's face, already beginning to wrinkle. Never mind, trust to chance—keep a sharp look out.— There is many a happy slave——'

In November 1838 Darwin visited the Wedgwoods at Maer Hall for the third time since his voyage. On the fourth day of this visit his cousin Emma and he found themselves alone in Uncle Joe's library. They were first cousins who had known each other from childhood. In the summer of 1838 their friendship had deepened. But Charles, being of the opinion that his face was 'repellently plain', had strong misgivings about Emma's feelings for him. His courage, however, won the day and he proposed.

To Emma who thought that her friendship with Charles might continue in a platonic sort of way for years, his proposal came as a great surprise. In a letter to one of her aunts she declared that although 'I knew how much I liked him, I was not in the least sure of his feelings, as he is so affectionate, and so fond of Maer and all of us, and demonstrative in his manners, that I did not think it meant anything . . .'. She accepted immediately and at Charles' request the wedding was fixed for 29 January 1839. By dint of much hunting and the help of Charles' brother Erasmus, a terraced house was found in London, near to Charles' favourite haunts, the British Museum and the Zoo.

The wedding over Charles and Emma left Shrewsbury by train for London taking with them sandwiches and a bottle of water (Charles did not drink wine). Emma's wealthy father had given her £5,000 and an annuity of £400. We have reason to believe that this generosity was more than matched by Charles'

father, for when Robert Peel reintroduced income tax in 1842 at
the rate of 7*d*. in the £ Darwin estimated that he would have to
pay £30 p.a.! But Darwin was pathologically worried about being
poor, and when he unloaded his troubled mind to his father, all
the Doctor would reply was 'stuff and nonsense!' Hence the rich
couple planned no exotic honeymoon. Instead they went straight
to No. 12, Upper Gower Street, one mile from Erasmus' house.
This was to be their home for the next two and a half years.

4

ON THE ORIGIN OF SPECIES

DARWIN's most important occupation during the twenty years
from 1839 to 1859 was the preparation of his case for the launch-
ing of evolution by natural selection. He knew that the time was
not ripe for this theory in 1839, and he had a horror of presenting
a theory without adducing adequate facts in its support. So for
these twenty years he busied himself fact-hunting and marshalling
the evidence thus obtained. At the same time he was anxious to
avoid prejudice in the selection of evidence, so he resisted de-
liberately the temptation to write even the briefest sketch of his
theory. 'In June 1842 I first allowed myself the satisfaction of
writing a very brief abstract of my theory in pencil in 35 pages;
and this was enlarged during the summer of 1844 into one of
230 pages, which I had fairly copied out and still possess.'

In these two essays Darwin gave apt illustrations of how he
believed natural selection was at work, and he discussed at some
length the nature and causes of variation. In the case of natural
selection he could not point to a single observed case, but he could
argue from circumstantial evidence that natural checks to population increase do exist. 'Suppose,' he said, 'in a certain spot there
are eight pairs of birds, and that only four pairs of them annually
(including double hatches) rear only four young, and that these
go on rearing their young at the same rate, then at the end of

seven years (a short life, excluding violent deaths, for any bird) there will be 2,048 birds, instead of the original sixteen.' But as no such increase is observed in nature we are driven to conclude that many birds die long before the seven years assumed here. Strong checks to the population increase of this bird must therefore exist. 'The same calculation applied to all animals and plants,' Darwin claimed, 'affords results more or less striking.'

Accepting that a struggle for existence does occur, how can it account for the production of organisms suited (adapted) to their conditions of life? The answer is simple: most variation, according to Darwin, is haphazard, i.e. whether the new variety is stronger or weaker, more prolific or less prolific, lighter skinned or darker skinned, &c., is purely a matter of chance—it is fortuitous—and bears no relation to the conditions of life. The struggle for existence acts like a sieve, discarding the poor varieties (i.e. the ill adapted) and leaving the strong varieties (i.e. the well adapted) to survive and multiply.

Unfortunately Darwin did not state that all variation is fortuitous. He had to be cautious because he was not sure of his ground when it came to the subject of variation. Precious little was known about variation and inheritance at the time and what good information there was Darwin seemed to ignore. The result was that he sat on the fence declaring himself both for *fortuitous* variation and for some *directed* variation of the kind Lamarck had favoured before him (see p. 21), and when his work came under attack in the 1860s he retreated farther and farther in the direction of Lamarck's theory of variation (see p. 58).

We also have to ask in what way the struggle for life can contribute to the production of different species from a single stock. This is the problem of the *divergence* or branching out of one original stock into several species. First, he believed that variation is accumulated providing it confers an advantage in the struggle for life. An organism which at first differs slightly from its parents can lead to descendants showing a more marked difference. Second, he accepted what was generally known at the time, namely that if a region is *isolated* from other regions by sea, mountains, rivers, and the like, new varieties have a greater chance of becoming established and of increasing their divergence because breeding with the normal type in neighbouring areas is unlikely. And even when there are no such barriers the struggle for life will favour divergence. It drives organisms to seek fresh shelter and protection in fresh situations and food from fresh sources. Further variations advantageous in these fresh habitats are thereby preserved and added to what is already there. The result is *indefinite divergence*.

Although Darwin seemed so unhurried about publication there is no doubt that in 1844 he regarded the second essay as his most important contribution to science, for at that time he wrote a letter to Emma asking her in the event of his sudden death to find an editor who for the sum of £400 would correct and enlarge it and see it through the press.

At the time of his marriage Darwin's closest friends were the Lyells and the Henslows. About two months after their marriage the Darwins entertained the Lyells, Henslows, the botanist Robert Brown, and the geologist Dr. Fitton to dinner. Emma described the occasion to her sister as follows: 'We had some time to wait before dinner for Dr. Fitton, which is always awful, and, in my opinion Mr. Lyell is enough to flatten a party, as he never speaks above his breath, so that everybody keeps lowering their tone to his. Mr. Brown, whom Humboldt calls "the glory of Great Britain" looks so shy, as if he longed to shrink into himself and disappear entirely; however not withstanding these two dead weights, viz.—the greatest botanist and the greatest geologist in Europe, we did very well and had no pauses. Mrs. Henslow has a good, loud, sharp voice which was a great comfort, and Mrs. Lyell has a very constant supply of talk. Mr. Henslow was very glad to meet Mr. Brown, as the two great botanists had a great deal to say to each other. Charles was dreadfully exhausted when it was over, and is only as well as can be expected today.' Why should a dinner party with his closest friends make him so ill? According to Darwin it was the excitement of such an occasion which put him into high spirits; he became animated, laughed with resounding peals, at the same time bringing his hands down with a hearty slap; he entered into the pleasure of the occasion and the good humour of his friends as one might expect of so sympathetic and good-natured a man. But the aftermath was awful—extreme lassitude, violent shivering, dizziness, and vomiting! Yet with all this his face retained its ruddy colour and gentle sympathetic expression throughout his life. Only his high forehead showed the many wrinkles of pain. Hence it is small wonder that his friends thought he was a hypochondriac. Despairingly he wrote to Hooker: 'Every one tells me that I look quite blooming and beautiful; and most think I am shamming...'

A number of Darwin's biographers have discussed this mysterious illness which no doctor of the day could diagnose and no water treatment, not even Dr. Gully's new cold-water treatment, could cure. At one time the opinion was rife that he was a hypochondriac. More recently it has been suggested that he was a sufferer from South American Trypanosomiasis, also known as Chaga's disease. The Trypanosome responsible is carried by the Benchuca bug of the Pampas, and we know that Darwin was bitten by this bug and was very ill afterwards. But he showed no signs of the progressive heart weakness which should have developed had he been a sufferer from this parasite. His involuntary nervous system showed the sort of disturbances characteristic of Chaga's disease, but they were present long before he was bitten. Professor Woodruff has examined the evidence in detail and his verdict on the Benchuca bug was 'Not Guilty'. For no one suffering from progressive heart disease could have walked so far or lived so long as did Darwin. At one time Darwin, who was very addicted to snuff, kept his snuff-box in the cellar and the key to it in the garret. To a man with a weak heart this would surely have prevented snuff-taking altogether!

It seems much more likely that the affliction was psychosomatic, i.e. an agitated nervous state which had disturbing effects on the functioning of the body's organs. The involuntary nervous system was the pathway by which this agitated mental state affected the muscles of the gut, the sensation of balance, the tone of skeletal muscles, and the sensation of tiredness. The results were nausea, flatulence, trembling of hands, a swimming feeling of the head, and excessive lassitude coupled with insomnia.

Undoubtedly Darwin took too much notice of his medical state, and in the end he became obsessed with it, keeping a health diary in which he recorded how good or bad his nights were and adding up the 'score' at the end of each week, but his stress symptoms were genuine.

Psychosomatic conditions of this sort are known to manifest themselves at varying ages. In Darwin's case there was a hint of such trouble at the age of twenty-two when he feared that it would be pointless for him to go on the *Beagle* voyage against his father's will for 'my father disliking would take away all energy'. And we have already noted (p. 18) the 'palpitations and pain around the heart' which he experienced as he waited impatiently for the sailing of the *Beagle*. The trouble cropped up again while he was a bachelor in London. Fondly he hoped that marriage could put an end to it, but alas, his afflictions grew steadily worse. Emma, who was a gay social type used to plenty of parties at Maer Hall and visits to the theatre and concert hall, seems to have accepted a quiet life in the interests of her husband's health. Gradually the visits to friends and attendance at scientific gatherings became less and less frequent. Emma became more and more the nurse, and Charles the patient. Indeed, Darwin's illness so dominated affairs at Down House that recently Dr. Hubble quipped, 'The perfect nurse had married the perfect patient.'

Darwin suffered so much in the years 1839–42 that he did less scientific work then than at any other time during his life. His work as Secretary to the Geological Society from 1837 to 1841 was, of course, partly to blame. In the hope that the quiet of the countryside would bring him peace and relief he began to think seriously about getting out of London. In 1842 Charles and Emma began the tedious task of house-hunting. When they had nearly despaired of finding anything suitable they came upon a plain Georgian house with eighteen acres of land called Down House, near the village of Downe. It was a square brick building covered with shabby whitewash and hanging tiles, and set deep in the chalk country of Kent. By this time they were desperate, so with Dr. Darwin's approval and money the purchase of Down

House from the Vicar of Downe was duly completed and in September 1842 the Darwins took possession.

In this rather bleak spot a quarter of a mile from the nearest village, eight and a half miles from the nearest railway station (Sydenham) and sixteen miles from St. Paul's Darwin spent the remaining forty years of his life. His good intention to go 'to town for a night every fortnight or three weeks' soon crumbled after the first few tedious and uncomfortable journeys which led to the usual stress symptoms. Apart from visits to Shrewsbury and to Maer Hall, to the British Association meetings, and to Dr. Gully's health establishment at Malvern and to Dr. Lane's 'delightful hydropathic establishment at Moor Park', he rarely ventured beyond the immediate surroundings of Downe. The 1855 meeting of the British Association at Glasgow was the last he ever attended. His longest absence from Downe was for sixteen weeks, all of which he spent under the care of Dr. Gully at Malvern (see Plate 7a).

Down House suited Darwin admirably. It was quiet, remote, and rural. By building high flint walls, purchasing additional land, and by the judicious planting of trees and shrubs he converted this estate into a haven. There he lived the life of a wealthy scientist and botanical experimenter, the house being run by a loyal team of servants led by the faithful Joseph Parslow who had been Darwin's butler in London.

At Downe, Darwin developed to the full the regular pattern of life which his tidy habits demanded. He rarely slept well and always awoke early; up he got and out he went into the morning air. Often the dawn was still breaking and the fox returning to his lair when the regular tap of Darwin's stick was heard on the path. The day's programme had started: Breakfast 7.45, work 8, letters and reading aloud from a novel 9.30, work 10.30, walk 12.15, lunch 1, newspaper and letter writing 2, rest and novel 3, walk 4, in drawing-room with family 5.30, rest and novel 6, dinner followed by two games of backgammon 7.30. Darwin's son Francis recalled that his father considered his work over by midday 'and would often say in a satisfied voice, "I've done a good day's work." ' The walk which followed was the longest of

D

the day. Usually it involved a fixed number of turns round the half-acre plot which he had stocked with trees and bordered with a sandy path. This delectable spot, known as the 'sand-walk' was the favourite haunt of the children as well as of their father. Sometimes the midday walk would take Darwin outside the grounds of Down House to the nearby woods, and especially to 'Orchis Bank', above Cudham valley where the orchids he so loved were plentiful, or to 'Hangrove Wood' where he enjoyed collecting grasses.

Adopting a regular pattern of life and keeping detailed records of it seem to have been a passion with Darwin throughout his life. As a young sportsman he recalled how he kept the score of the gamebirds he shot by making knots in a piece of string tied to a button-hole. Now in his thirties at Downe he kept a record of how many circuits he made of the sand-walk ($\frac{1}{3}$ mile per circuit) by kicking a flint across the path for each completed turn. This delight in recording events was undoubtedly an asset to him in his scientific work.

Darwin's fear that he might 'turn into a complete Kentish hog' at Downe was well justified. That he did not is due to his zeal in letter writing and reading of current scientific literature. It mattered not who wrote to him; he always replied. He worked at foreign languages until he could read books in German, French, and Latin. No matter how difficult the style, if he thought the matter relevant he ploughed through it. In the exchange of ideas and information this absence of a language barrier is of vital importance to a scientist. But no amount of reading and writing could really keep him in touch with the scientific chit-chat of London or give him an adequate picture of that very elusive thing the 'climate of opinion'. His two closest friends, Charles Lyell and Joseph Hooker, did more to keep him in touch than anyone else, but as we shall see their influence was not enough. As a botanist Hooker was of greater help on technical matters, but for the development of the fundamental idea of evolution by natural selection Lyell had the greater influence.

The friendship between Lyell and Darwin developed as a result of Darwin's coral island theory. 'I was greatly surprised and encouraged,' Darwin recalled, 'by the vivid interest which he [Lyell] showed. On such occasions, while absorbed in thought, he would throw himself into the strangest attitudes, often resting his head on the seat of a chair, while standing up.[1] His delight in science was ardent, and he felt the keenest interest in the future progress of mankind.' Above all else he was very kind to Darwin, and knowing his faults he did his best to make him overcome them. It was Lyell who persuaded Darwin to publish a preliminary sketch of his coral island theory, and it was Lyell who tried to pump some courage and sense of urgency into his reluctant and procrastinating friend over the publication of his species work. In 1856 he warned him about the possibility of being anticipated, and in this connexion he drew Darwin's attention to a paper by Alfred Russel Wallace, entitled, 'On the law that has regulated the introduction of new species', which appeared in 1855. Wallace wrote this paper when he was in Sarawak when he had become convinced that as one species dies out another arises in its place, but he had no idea how.

Lyell must have given Darwin quite a strong lecture on the 'publish or die' theme, for Darwin wrote in agitated terms to Hooker for his advice. He explained that a contribution to a scientific journal was out of the question, for such a publication might bring abuse upon the editor. But the real trouble was that Darwin just could not bear naked speculation. His own grandfather, Erasmus Darwin, had speculated wildly, and look where that had got him! His contemporary Coleridge coined the term 'darwinizing' to imply empty speculation! No, the evidence must be supplied at the same time as the theory. But what a task it was to collect evidence for so broad a theory. Lyell feared that his friend would never publish his work. The notes would go on piling up and the task of abstracting them would become more and more difficult.

Darwin was also unduly fearful that his work if published would bring abuse and savage criticism upon his head. The origin of species was a far more dangerous topic than the origin of coral

---

[1] After a splendid talk with Lyell in 1861 Darwin said: 'He was many times on his knees, with elbows on the sofa.'

islands or of the Cordillera. When he admitted to Hooker that he was an evolutionist he said it was 'like committing a murder'. We can only understand this attitude if we remember that his wife, Emma, his teachers, Sedgwick and Henslow, and his former employer, Fitz-Roy, were all devout Christians; Henslow and Sedgwick, his cousin Fox, and his friend Leonard Jenyns were all in holy orders. They did not reflect the thinking of a younger generation either in the universities or in other walks of life. Had Darwin visited London more often he might have realized that times had changed since his Cambridge days in the twenties. Lyell's *Principles* had had a decisive impact on geologists by the late forties and was also affecting biological opinion. Meanwhile the anonymous work *The Vestiges of the History of Creation* had appeared. It had been reviewed savagely by Sedgwick and Huxley. 'Woe to the world,' cried Sedgwick, 'if our knowledge is to be made up of idle speculations, like those we have just been reviewing.' Its authorship had been hotly disputed and it had sold so well that few educated Englishmen were ignorant of the Lamarckian ideas its author advanced.

The savage treatment meted out to 'Mr. Vestiges' only served to confirm Darwin's fears of the consequences of publishing. These fears were still prominent in 1856 when he tried to write a preliminary sketch of his theory. 'I tremble about it,'[1] he wrote to his cousin Fox, 'which I should not do, if I allowed some three or four more years to elapse before publishing anything . . . my notes are so numerous during nineteen years' collecting, that it would take me at least a year to go over and classify them.' Four months later he had given up his attempt at the preliminary sketch, and instead was preparing a full abstract. In November he was beginning to fear that he would break down, for his subject was getting 'bigger and bigger with each month's work'. In no time at all it was 1858. He was still making slow progress despite working very hard (presumably two and a half hours per

[1] As late as 1860 he was worrying about the difficulties of 'explaining' particular structures—the peacock's tail feather made him feel sick, and he recalled how the thought of the [structure of the] eye used to make him feel 'cold all over'. These admissions show that he had a proper appreciation of the difficulties his theory had raised.

day), 'perhaps too hard', he said. 'It will be very big, and I am become deeply interested in the way facts fall into groups. I am like Croesus overwhelmed with my riches in facts, and I mean to make my book as perfect as ever I can. I shall not go to press at soonest for a couple of years.'

Meanwhile Alfred Russel Wallace was still far away in the Malay Archipelago and still deeply interested in the question of the origin of species. In February 1858, when he was suffering from an intermittent fever which necessitated lying down for several hours every day, his mind went back to his reading of Malthus twelve years before. He remembered the impressive accounts of 'the positive checks to increase' which keep down the population of savage races. Then he asked himself: 'Why do some die and some live?' And the answer was clearly, 'That on the whole the best fitted live . . . Then it suddenly flashed upon me that this self-acting process would necessarily *improve the race*, because in every generation the inferior would be killed off and the superior would remain—that is, *the fittest would survive*'. At once he saw how potent selection would be when the conditions of life changed. Before his fit of fever was over he had thought it out almost completely. The moment he got up he began to write it down, and as far as he could remember the first draft was finished the next day. Before the end of that week he had copied out the final draft on thin letter paper and sent it off to Darwin!

Poor Darwin; he had corresponded with Wallace and had congratulated him on his paper of 1855. 'I believe I go much further than you,' he wrote in December 1857, 'but it is too long a subject to enter on my speculative notions.' If only he had divulged his secret to Wallace then. Now his hands were tied. What was he to do? Lyell's warning had come true 'with a vengeance'. So to Lyell he wrote for advice. 'I never saw a more striking coincidence; if Wallace had my MS. sketch written out in 1842, he could not have made a better short abstract! Even his terms now stand as heads to my chapters. Please return me the MS., which he does not say he wishes me to publish, but I shall, of course, at once write and offer to send to any journal. So all my originality will be smashed . . .' After a week had passed he began to have second thoughts. Perhaps he could publish a selection of his earlier writings. To this suggestion Lyell and Hooker agreed. They arranged the whole affair, and on 1 July 1858 Wallace's paper and two extracts from Darwin's work, dated 1844 and September 1857 were read by Lyell and Hooker to the Linnean Society. The interest of the audience of thirty was intense, but there was no semblance of a discussion. Hooker felt that 'the subject was too novel and too ominous for the old school to enter the lists before armouring'. After the meeting it was talked over with bated breath: 'Lyell's approval, and perhaps in a small way, mine as his lieutenant in the affair, rather overawed the Fellows, who would otherwise have flown out against the doctrine.' But neither the awe nor the excitement lasted and in his Annual Report for 1858 the President of the Linnean Society stated that 'the year has not been marked by any such striking discoveries which at once revolutionize so to speak the department of science on which they bear . . .'. The only notice that Darwin could recall of the reading of these papers was by Professor Haughton of Dublin 'whose verdict was that all that was new in them was false, and what was true was not new'.

By this time Darwin had realized that his 'Big Book' or 'Abstract' of his notes was getting unwieldy. Lyell's fear that he never would publish it had been justified. So he dropped it and started a smaller work which was intended to form a series of papers to be published by the Linnean Society. But by the beginning of 1859 this 'Abstract of an Abstract' was clearly too big for any journal; it would have to be a book. In this circuitous manner his famous work, *On the origin of species by means of natural selection or the preservation of favoured races in the struggle for life*, was born. The arrangement of subject matter in the book is briefly: (1) variation under domestication and under nature; (2) the struggle for existence and natural selection; (3) difficulties of the theory; (4) explanatory powers of the theory —hybridization, geological record, geographical distribution, classification. By the spring of 1859, when the final corrections were being made, it was clearly going to make a book of about

500 pages. Through Lyell's good offices John Murray was persuaded to publish it. On 12 November 1859 it appeared and by the end of business that day all 1,250 copies had been sold.

One cannot *prove* that all living organisms have evolved under natural selection. Facts and laws can be established, but theories can only be rendered more probable or less probable by testing. Hence, even today, an act of faith is required to extend the principle from a few extremely probable cases to all species. But in 1859 Darwin could not even point to a single observed case 'in the wild'. He had to content himself with drawing analogies between what man has produced by *artificial* selection and what nature appears to have done by *natural* selection. His aim was to persuade the reader that his theory was more credible than the Creation Theory by showing that it explains more. The result was that the *Origin*, as its author remarked, 'is one long argument'; it reads like a legal case conducted on behalf of natural selection with the Creation Theory as the defendant. At the same time it contains no statement about the origin of life itself. Darwin left the way open for the Special Creationists to retreat to this point. He also left lines of retreat for himself, so that Samuel Butler, the philosopher and novelist, described the book as 'like the opinion of a lawyer who wanted to leave loopholes, or an Act of Parliament full of repealed and inserted clauses'.

No sooner was the *Origin* published than abuse poured down on Darwin's head. Sedgwick found much of the book false and mischievous. 'You have *deserted*,' he said, 'the true method of induction [i.e., drawing conclusions from facts established by observation.] . . . Many of your wide conclusions are based on assumptions which can neither be proved nor disproved, why then express them in the language of philosophical induction?' Other writers complained that they were not interested in what Darwin believed or was convinced of, but in what he could prove. He was criticized for many other things: for personifying natural selection, for the tone of triumphant confidence with which he ends the book, for explaining too much (a theory that explains everything being considered highly improbable), for the repeated use of the phrase 'my theory'. In 1861 D. H. Watson found the words 'I', 'me', 'my' forty-three times in the Introduction to the *Origin*. More recently Professor Darlington has pointed out that the phrase 'my theory', which appears forty-five times in the whole book, was altered to 'the theory' gradually through successive editions until in the last edition (1872) there was only one 'my theory' left. The chief cause of this change was an obscure Scottish botanist by the name of Patrick Mathew who complained that he had advanced the idea of natural selection more than twenty-nine years before Darwin. This initiated a debate over priority which led to the discovery of another precursor of Darwin —the surgeon William Charles Wells, and in 1959 to yet another —the geologist James Hutton. His brief discussion of the subject was first published in Sir Edward Bailey's book, *Charles Lyell* (Collins, 1962). Of these three writers the one who anticipated Darwin most closely was Mathew. 'He gives,' wrote Darwin to Wallace in 1860, '*most clearly* but very briefly . . . our view of Natural Science. It is a most complete case of anticipation.'

There is nothing strange about this fact. More often than not discoveries in science are made several times. But it was a great pity that Darwin failed to be generous in his written acknowledgements to either Mathew for his statement of natural selection or to Lamarck and his own grandfather, Erasmus Darwin, for their writings on evolution (without selection). All too often he spoke as if natural selection was the whole of evolution, whereas it is really only one ingredient. For these shortcomings Samuel Butler took him to task. The bitterness of these attacks by one who was formerly his admirer hurt Darwin sorely and eventually stunned him into silence.

Darwin was fifty when the *Origin* was published. Before he reached sixty the current of opinion had moved strongly in favour of evolution (i.e. the origin of species progressively one from another by a process of change) and to a lesser extent in favour of natural selection as the agent necessary for this process to take place. One of his greatest joys was the long-delayed conversion of Lyell, who until 1868 had believed that evolution proceeds by a series of large jumps, sudden changes of structure, what are now called macromutations. This belief which he had held privately since the 1830s became increasingly popular during the latter half of the nineteenth century; it did not rule out natural selection altogether but it greatly restricted its role. Darwin's friend, T. H. Huxley, played a major part in swinging the pendulum in favour of the evolutionists. While he fought Darwin's battles at public meetings and in the popular Press, Darwin stayed at home and contented himself with answering his critics in successive editions of the *Origin,* and in continuing his programme of biological experiments in the quiet of his garden at Downe.

After the first wave of outraged criticism and frivolous abuse had died down Darwin found his work subjected to criticism of a more serious nature. Do changes in the conditions of life really cause heritable variations? they asked. Are single variations swamped by crossing? Has the earth existed as long as your theory demands? In the face of these questions Darwin found his knowledge inadequate. He knew nothing of the work of the plant ecologist Franz Unger, which would have helped him to answer the first question, or of that of the plant hybridist Gregor Mendel, which would have provided him with the answer to the second, and he could know nothing about modern estimates of the age of the earth which would have saved him any embarrassment over the third.

Franz Unger (1800–70), Professor of Plant Physiology in the University of Vienna, had made a detailed study of a number of closely related plants, some of which are confined to acid rocks, and others to alkaline rocks. At first he thought it was the nature of the rocks which had caused these plants to vary and thus differ on different mountains. But after failing to find a chemical explanation of how such action might occur he denied it. Other botanists inspired by his example carried out more conclusive experiments, so that belief in a direct action of the external world in producing adaptations was seriously undermined. Faced with these results at the close of his life, Darwin remarked that if variation is really independent of the conditions of life, 'the astonishing variation of almost all cultivated plants must be due to selection and breeding from the varying individuals. This idea crossed my mind many years ago, but I was afraid to publish it, as I thought that people would say, "How he does exaggerate the importance of selection." '

Now if we inquire why Darwin continued to believe that it is the conditions of life which cause variation, several reasons suggest themselves. The letter of 1881 from which we have just quoted, points to over anxiety about the reception of his work, and we have already noted this trait in connexion with his excessive fears about publishing his work (see p. 52). A second reason was his acceptance of the blending theory of inheritance current at the time which likened fertilization to the mixing of ink and water. Differences are therefore blended, diluted, and in the course of time obliterated. How, then, is the supply of variation maintained? By every change in the conditions of life stimulating fresh variability.

The full implications of this blending theory were not brought home to Darwin until 1867 when a Scottish engineer named Fleeming Jenkin worked out the probability of the persistence of single variations. Then Darwin realized just how rarely they would be perpetuated. From then on he laid more and more emphasis on variation *stimulated* and *directed* by the conditions of life. Fleeming Jenkin's calculations were right, it was the blending theory which was wrong. Characters such as height in man, weight of bean seeds, &c., appear to blend, but is it true also that the *transmitters* of these characters blend? Darwin had collected plenty of evidence himself which showed that the transmitter of a character and its expression are quite distinct processes. These hereditary transmitters which make up the hereditary material of the sperm and the egg are particles which refuse to blend. And unknown to Darwin and the scientific world at large, the laws which govern their behaviour had been discovered by the Moravian monk, Gregor Mendel (1822–84), who published his now famous experiments on the garden pea in 1866. His work provided the basis for a sound understanding of the nature of inheritance and the way in which cross-breeding produces, not, as Darwin believed, uniformity, but variability. Hence it was not until Mendel's work was discovered in 1900 that evolution by natural selection became a satisfactory theory.

Darwin did not live to see this important revision of his work. Sadly he wrote to Huxley: 'The pendulum is now swinging against our side, but I feel positive it will soon swing the other way; . . . It will be a long battle, after we are dead and gone.'

We can now return to the quotation at the beginning of this book, '. . . my brain was never formed for much thinking'. Here was an extremely competent naturalist with a passionate curiosity who, by virtue of these qualities, hit upon evolution by natural selection. Unfortunately he was not richly endowed with the intellectual courage of a reformer and the brevity and lucidity of a natural writer, so the task of preparing his case became a terrible ordeal. It took him years, but he did it in the end, and for this achievement he is justly acclaimed a genius. But it was not the writing of the *Origin* which he recalled in later life with great pleasure but his studies of primrose and orchid flowers. These combined detailed observation with a novel explanation of the functions of the structures described. No long arguments, no involvement of the writer in disputations on metaphysics, just straight observation, hypothesis, experiment, and conclusion. There is not space in this brief biography to describe the many such topics which Darwin opened up so successfully. For an account of these the reader is referred to the more comprehensive works cited on p. 62.

In March 1882 Darwin took his last turn around his favourite sand-walk. By 18 April he had realized that the end was near and said: 'I am not the least afraid to die.' All next morning he felt very faint; at four o'clock he died. Among the ten pall-bearers who carried him to his grave in Westminster Abbey on the 26th were Wallace, Hooker, Huxley, and his opponent, the Duke of Argyle. Of his ten children seven survived him, together with Emma who died in 1896.

Although he had not met his father's wish by becoming a parson but had furthered the cause of agnosticism, to the grief of his devout wife, he still felt that he had acted rightly in steadily devoting his life to science. 'I feel,' he said, 'no remorse from having committed any great sin, but have often and often regretted that I have not done more direct good to my fellow creatures.'

PRINCIPAL DATES

1809   Born at Shrewsbury on 12 February at 'The Mount'.

1817   Death of his mother, Susannah (née Wedgwood).

1818   Entered Shrewsbury School.

1826   Spent one year at Edinburgh University and read his first two scientific papers to the Plinian Society.

1831   Received degree of B.A. for his studies at Cambridge University from 1828 to 1830. 27 December, departure of H.M.S. *Beagle* (for principal dates of the voyage, see Table I, p. 18).

1836   Anchored at Falmouth on 2 October.

1837   Moved to London on 13 March. Read the fifth edition of Lyell's *Principles*. Opened first Notebook on the Transmutation of Species in July. *Journal* completed in November.

1838   Read Malthus' *Essay on Population* in October and realized the significance of 'positive checks to increase'. Engaged to Emma Wedgwood on 11 November.

1839   Married at Maer on 29 January. Went to live in London. His *Journal* published in August.

1842   Wrote his first essay on the origin of species in May. Went to live at Downe in September.

1844   Wrote his second essay on the origin of species in June.

1848   Death of his father on 12 November. According to Sir Arthur Keith Darwin inherited approximately £45,000.

1849   Spent four months at Dr. Gully's establishment at Malvern.

1856   Lyell advised him to publish a sketch of his species theory, but Darwin started instead to write a big 'Abstract', which he started in May.

1858   Received Wallace's essay on 18 June. Joint Darwin–Wallace paper read to the Linnean Society 1 July. Began the *Origin* three weeks later.

1859   The *Origin* published 24 November. October–December at the water-cure establishment, Ilkley.

1865–71 The *Origin* was subjected to serious attacks: the age of the earth by Lord Kelvin, the swamping effect of crossing by Fleeming Jenkin, these and the genesis of complex structures by St. George Mivart.

1872   The sixth and final edition of the *Origin*.

1876   Wrote his *Autobiography*.

1881   Publication of, *The Formation of Vegetable Mold through the action of Earthworms,* his fifteenth and last book.

1882   Died at Down House on 19 April. Buried in Westminster Abbey beside Sir Isaac Newton on 26 April.

NOTES ON THE PLATES

1(*a*).   This illustration was found by Dr. Tellwright in the Estate Records. He describes it as a small part of a plan of the estate printed on canvas. This spelling (Mere) of the Hall is no longer used.

7(*a*).   Dr. Gully brought his water-cure to Malvern in 1842–3 and built two embattled buildings, the Tudor House for women and the Holyrood House for men. This illustration is taken from a Victorian notepaper heading and shows Tudor House from the garden side and on the right a part of Holyrood House with the 'Bridge of Sighs' connecting the two buildings. The buildings now form the Tudor Hotel.

FOR FURTHER READING

THE most compact biography of Darwin is by Francis Darwin, (ed.) *Charles Darwin: his life told in an autobiographical chapter and in a selected series of his published letters* (Murray, 1902). A biography with emphasis on the domestic and personal aspects of life at Down House is Sir Arthur Keith, *Darwin revalued* (Watts, 1955). For the nature of Darwin's illness see: Professor Woodruff, 'Darwin's health in relation to his voyage to South America', *Brit. Med. J.*, 1 (1965), 745–50. Darwin's Autobiography was published in full by Nora Barlow, *The Autobiography of Charles Darwin 1809–1882 with original omissions restored . . .* (Collins, 1958, also as a paperback in Collier Books, 1961), and also by Lady Barlow, *Charles Darwin's Diary of the voyage of H.M.S. 'Beagle'. Edited from the MS.* (Cambridge University Press, 1934), and *Darwin–Henslow Correspondence* (Murray, in press). Three excellent reprints of Darwin's two most popular works are: *Voyage of the Beagle* (Bantam Paperbacks and Everyman Paperbacks), *On the Origin of Species* 1st edn, with a Foreword by C. D. Darlington (Watts, 1950), 6th edn, with a Foreword by Sir Julian Huxley (Mentor Books, 1958). Professor Darlington's Foreword is a brilliant piece of writing and provides a succinct account of the part played by the *Origin* in the growth of ideas. An exposition of Darwinian theory is provided by A. R. Wallace, *Darwinism . . .* (Macmillan, 1889), and a recent assessment by P. R. Bell (ed.), *Darwin's biological work: some aspects reconsidered* (Cambridge University Press, 1959). For comprehensive accounts of Darwin and his work, see Sir Gavin de Beer, *Charles Darwin* (Nelson, 1963), and Julian Huxley and H. B. D. Kettlewell, *Charles Darwin and his world* (Thames & Hudson, 1965). The latter contains the best collection of plates. Darwin's debt to his predecessors and his Lamarckian retreat are described in Loren Eiseley, *Darwin's Century: Evolution and the men who discovered it* (Gollancz, 1959), C. D. Darlington, *Darwin's place in history* (Blackwell, 1960), and Sydney Smith, 'The origin of "The Origin"', *Advancement of Sci.*, No. 64 (1960), 391–401.

INDEX